THE 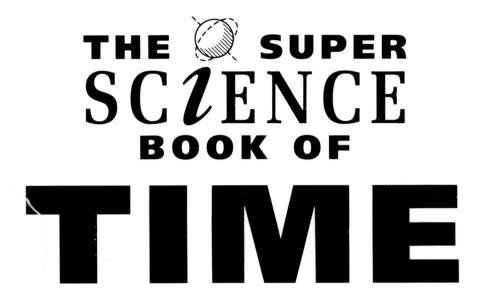 SUPER SCIENCE BOOK OF TIME

Kay Davies and Wendy Oldfield

The Clever Clock

There's a battered old clock in the garden shed,
It's filthy and tired and definitely dead.
Its weights are missing, its cuckoo flown,
Its cogs are rusty and the spring is blown.

Spiders live in the cuckoo's nest,
There's no doubt about it, it's past its best.
But twice a day come rain, come shine,
Its ancient fingers point the right time.

Illustrations by Frances Lloyd

Thomson Learning
New York

Titles in the Super Science series

Light
Our Bodies
Time
Weather

First published in the
United States in 1993 by
Thomson Learning
115 Fifth Avenue
New York, NY 10003

First published in 1992 by
Wayland (Publishers) Ltd

Library of Congress Cataloging-in-Publication Data applied for

ISBN: 1-56847-020-7
Printed in Italy

Series Editor: Cally Chambers
Designer: Loraine Hayes Design

Picture acknowledgments

Illustrations by Frances Lloyd.
Cover illustration by Martin Gordon.

Photographs by permission of: J. Allan Cash 7; Cephas 15 top;
Bruce Coleman Ltd . 11 (Rydell), 16 (Pott), 17 top (Taylor) 18
top (Taylor), 19; Eye Ubiquitous 26; Michael Holford 13;
PHOTRI 22; Tony Stone Worldwide 5, 12, 15 bottom 18
bottom, 20; Topham 29 top; Wayland Picture Library 9
(Zul Mukhida); Werner Forman Archive 23, 25; ZEFA 4,
17 bottom group, 18 middle. Reproduced by permission of
the trustees of the Science Museum 29 bottom.

CONTENTS

TIMES PAST

Ask people who are older than you what things they remember from the time before you were born. They will tell you about both happy and sad memories of times gone by.

▲ Many people like to collect things such as stamps, old coins, matchboxes, or picture cards. These have stories to tell too. Their pictures and words can be interesting and funny. They can tell us about times past. What is the oldest coin in your pocket? Can a stamp tell you about famous people? Do you laugh at pictures of the clothes people used to wear?

◄ Perhaps you have family photographs. Some may be quite old. The faded brown pictures can tell you about your family from a long time ago.

ANCIENT HISTORY

The earth is very old. It is changing all the time. New rocks are forming and old mountains are being worn away. Earth's history lies in the rocks.

▲ The Grand Canyon is a deep gorge that has been cut by the Colorado River. Climbing down into the canyon, past the layers of rock, is like taking a journey back through time. The oldest rock at the bottom is about 2 billion years old. Fossils found in the rock layers make it possible to tell their age.

Through the ages people have left behind lots of clues about their lives. Archaeologists are scientists who spend their time digging for these clues. They can tell a lot just from finding trash, tools, and the foundations of people's homes. Pottery, glass, coins, and even bones are valuable to them in building a picture of how people used to live. Even in our own backyards we can sometimes find evidence of people who lived there before us.

Fossils found in many parts of the world show that humans are quite new to the planet. We have only been around for about half a million years.

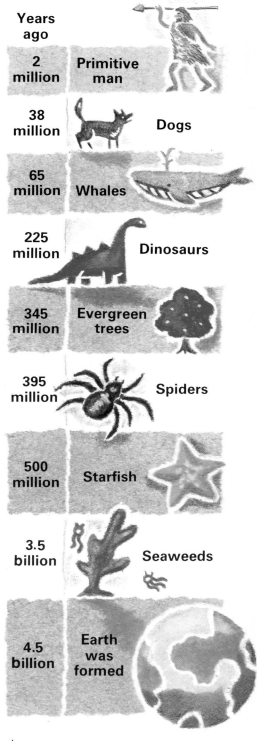

Years ago	
2 million	Primitive man
38 million	Dogs
65 million	Whales
225 million	Dinosaurs
345 million	Evergreen trees
395 million	Spiders
500 million	Starfish
3.5 billion	Seaweeds
4.5 billion	Earth was formed

▲This simple timeline shows just how young the human race is. Look at how old some other plant and animal species are.

ON TIME

Do you wear a watch? Is it just a piece of jewelry or do you look at it often? Time is important to nearly everyone in a busy world. Most people have some sort of clock in their homes and many homes have lots of clocks. Some tell us the time of day. Some tell our ovens, video machines or hot-water systems when to switch on or off.

We check the time often so that we can catch buses or trains, be on time for school, do our shopping, or watch our favorite television program. Clocks help us run our lives. They help us to organize our own time and to coordinate with other people.

Picture Clock

◀ Draw a clock face that shows some of the things you do at the same time every day. You might include meal times, schooltime, playtime, and bedtime.

BODY CLOCK

We don't always need to look at a clock to tell the time. Our bodies have their own built-in clocks. When we get used to a daily routine, our body clocks can be very accurate. They can tell us when it's time to wake up, to eat, or to go to sleep.

Many animals get so used ▶ to feeding at a regular time that their bodies work like clocks. If we put food out for birds and animals, they soon get to know when it will be there. They begin to wait for it. Ducks have even been known to cross busy roads with their babies for a regular meal.

If we do the same thing often enough, such as going home or having dinner at the same time every day, our bodies can learn to judge set periods of time. But if we are scared, bored, or looking forward to something, a few minutes can seem like hours. When we're enjoying ourselves, time can pass quickly and hours fly by like minutes.

HERE COMES THE SUN!

Ancient peoples had no real clocks to tell them the time. They had to rely on the sun, the moon, and the seasons to tell them how time was passing. They got up when the sun rose and worked while there was light to see by.

The sun was so important in people's lives that it was often thought of as a god. People made up stories to explain why the sun rose and set each day.

The Vikings of Scandinavia believed that the sun and the moon traveled through the sky in chariots pulled by horses. Each was followed by a fierce, hungry wolf. Neither charioteer dared stop even for a second, for both feared they would be eaten.

DAY AND
NIGHT

The light from some stars takes thousands of years to reach us. The sun is Earth's nearest star. Its light takes 8.3 minutes to reach Earth. The sun gives out heat too. Without the sun, our planet would be dark, cold, and lifeless.

▲ The earth is an enormous globe. It travels around the sun, spinning as it goes. The earth takes twenty-four hours —one day—to spin around once. It spins from west to east, so each morning the sun appears in the eastern sky. We call this sunrise. During daylight hours the sun seems to move across the sky as the earth turns. Finally it sets in the west. Night falls as that part of the earth's surface turns away from the sun and passes into shadow. At the same time on the other side of the world, a new day is beginning.

▲ You can see for yourself how day follows night across the world. Ask a friend to shine a flashlight on a globe or ball in a darkened room. Turn the globe slowly from west to east.

WOW!
On the planet Venus your classes would last a long time. It spins so slowly that one day there lasts for 243 Earth days.

LIVING BY DAY

All living things have a time to be active and a time to rest. Most people work during daylight hours and sleep after dark. Others work at night, providing things like emergency services or entertainment.

Many plants and animals are active during the daytime. Some flowers are so sensitive to daylight that they open and close at certain times each day. In fact, they can be so accurate that the eighteenth-century scientist, Carl Linnaeus, showed how they could be used to tell the time in a floral clock like this. ▶

Bees, and other insects that visit light-sensitive flowers to collect nectar, soon learn when they will be open. When the flowers close, the insects are not attracted to them, and they move on to other types of plants while daylight lasts.

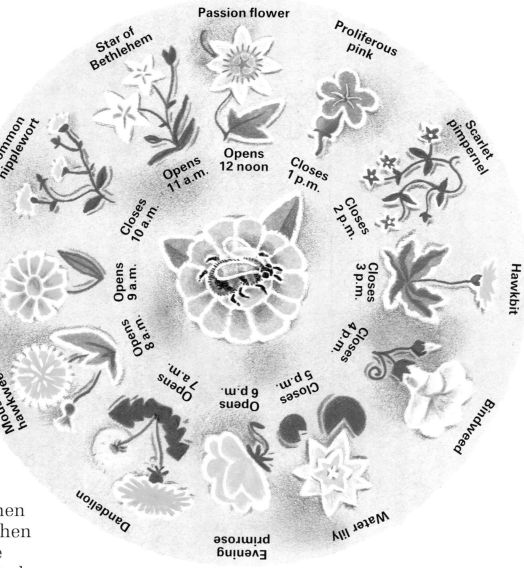

Passion flower
Star of Bethlehem
Proliferous pink
Common nipplewort
Scarlet pimpernel
Opens 11 a.m.
Opens 12 noon
Closes 1 p.m.
Closes 10 a.m.
Closes 2 p.m.
Field marigold
Opens 9 a.m.
Closes 3 p.m.
Hawkbit
Opens 8 a.m.
Closes 4 p.m.
Mouse ear hawkweed
Opens 7 a.m.
Opens 6 p.m.
Closes 5 p.m.
Bindweed
Dandelion
Evening primrose
Water lily

▲ A floral clock can only be accurate in a small area because light and other growing conditions vary with the region. In summer, you could investigate the flowers near you and make a floral clock like this one.

NIGHT LIFE

When the sun goes down, the creatures of the night come out. Owls, bats, and foxes are out hunting. Each of these animals is specially adapted for night living. Some have good night vision, others have sharp hearing or a strong sense of smell.

Some flowers, like honeysuckle, open at night. Their powerful scent attracts moths to drink the nectar. The moths risk being eaten by bats. Bats have a built-in echo location system that makes them excellent night hunters. Squeaking as they fly, bats listen for the echoes to bounce back off things around them.

▲ Squeaks bouncing off a moth tell the bat exactly where it is. The hunting bat swoops in to snatch it. The moth's survival kit is its sensitive hearing. Its ears catch the squeaks of the hunting bat. If it is quick enough, the moth can escape by suddenly dropping to the ground or swerving. Some moths can even squeak back and confuse the bat.

▲ As the sun rises, bats return to their caves to sleep away the day.

M O V I N G
SHADOWS

The sun itself makes a good, simple clock. Its light casts shadows on the earth. The shadows change in length and direction through the day as the earth turns. Shadows can give us a guide to the passage of time.

In the early morning the sun casts ▶ long shadows pointing westwards. As the sun rises in the sky, the shadows gradually get shorter until midday, when the sun is at its highest. After midday they grow again, but this time they point eastwards.

Cat and Mouse

1 Find a window that catches lots of sunlight for most of the day.
2 Tape an "X" on the window and watch how the shadow on the wall or floor moves for a day.

3 Draw and cut out the shapes of a cat and a mouse.
4 Tape the cat on the window.
5 Tape your mouse on the wall or floor so that the cat's shadow chases the mouse all day and finally catches it in the evening.

SHADOW CLOCKS

The very first clocks made use of shadows to divide the day into equal time periods. A marker was used to cast a shadow onto a dial as the sun moved across the sky. The ancient Egyptians, Greeks, Romans, and Chinese all developed sundials and were able to use them quite accurately.

This Italian sundial cube was painted ▶ in about 1560 and was only accurate in Florence. The cube was made with five different faces so that the time could be read in any of the three time systems that were used in those days.

Today, we still see sundials that tell us the time on their curved scales. Shadow clocks and sundials help chart the passing of time, but they are only useful when the sun is shining.

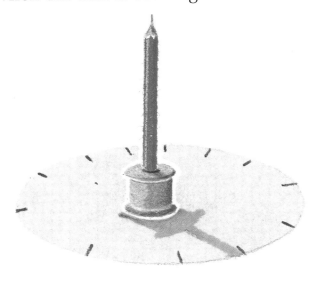

Make Your Own Sun Clock
1 Fix a pencil into a threaded spool or lump of clay.
2 Stand it in the center of a piece of cardboard and place the cardboard on a windowsill that catches the sun all day.
3 Mark the shadow and time on the cardboard, every hour.
4 Put the cardboard in the same position and use the shadow clock to tell the time on the next sunny day.

THE SEASONS

The earth is an enormous ball of rock spinning in space. It travels around the sun in a huge loop, called its orbit. Each orbit takes one year to complete.

The earth spins around on its axis. This ▶ is a line that passes through the earth from the North Pole to the South Pole. Halfway between the poles, on the earth's surface, is the equator. This divides the earth into two halves called hemispheres.

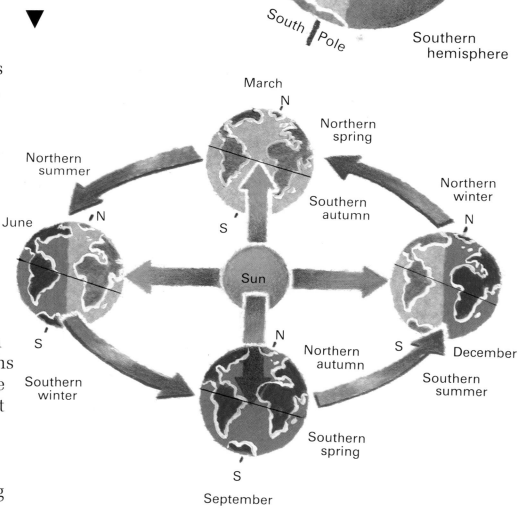

Earth's axis is tilted. It always leans in the same direction. Earth's tilt and its position on its orbit around the sun give the world its seasons. The seasons change as each half of the earth leans at an angle toward or away from the sun. In June the Northern Hemisphere leans toward the sun. It is summer there and winter in the Southern Hemisphere. Six months later the earth is on the other side of the sun. It is then winter in the Northern Hemisphere and summer south of the equator. The spring and autumn months occur in between winter and summer when the earth is part way around its annual orbit.

DAWN TO DUSK

In northern and southern parts of the world we expect spring to come each year, followed by summer, autumn, and winter. We look forward to the long, hot days of summer. Winters are not always as fun. Dusk comes early. Nights are long and often cold. We get up in the dark, and daylight hours are short.

In lands around the poles, the sun doesn't rise at all in winter. For six months, dawn never comes. The icy wastelands are covered in darkness.

Places near the equator never tilt away from the sun and so do not have four clear seasons. Days and nights are almost the same length all year round and seasonal changes may only be marked by more or less rainfall.

▲　At the poles, the sun is below the horizon for six months of darkness and above the horizon for six months of daylight.

◄　Many people in southern Australia spend Christmas Day on a hot beach.

SEASONAL JOURNEYS

As days grow longer and warmer, summertime arrives. In many parts of the world, birds fly in from colder places. They come to build nests and raise their young on the many insects that can be found in the warm conditions. Their natural body clocks tell them when to come to their regular summer lands and when to leave again. They may use the sun, the stars, and the earth's magnetic field to guide them on their long journeys.

Even insects make long journeys. Monarch butterflies breed in Canada. Most fly south to spend winter in the warmth of Mexico.

▲ Many mammals migrate too. Caribou are a type of deer. They travel up to 800 miles to spend the summer months grazing in the Arctic. Each autumn they trek south again to cold but sheltered forests, where they can find enough food for the winter.

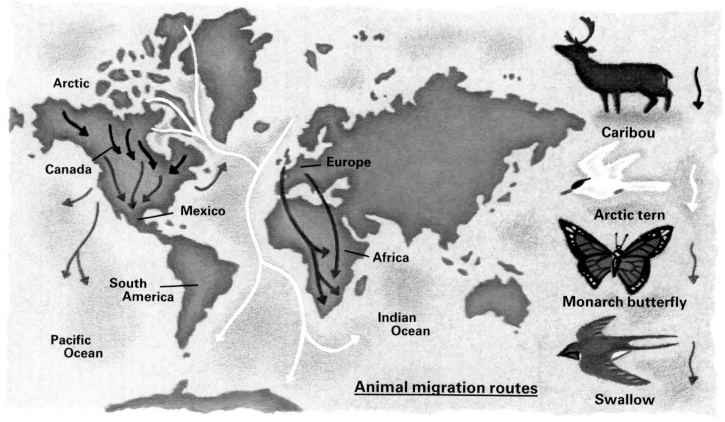

Arctic

Canada

Mexico

Europe

Africa

South America

Indian Ocean

Pacific Ocean

Animal migration routes

Caribou

Arctic tern

Monarch butterfly

Swallow

WINTER'S SLEEP

Winter can be a difficult time for many animals. They have to work hard to find food and keep warm. The weakest may not survive.

Some animals, like woodchucks and dormice, spend the winter in hibernation. In summer they eat and eat to build up reserves of fat to live off during winter. As the days shorten they become sleepy. When the air becomes colder their body temperature drops. Their heartbeat and breathing slow. Gently they fall into a deep sleep that lasts all winter.

▲ This dormouse has made a soft and warm nest in which to hibernate.

Winter

Spring

Autumn

Summer

WOW!
Only one bird hibernates. The whippoorwill of North America finds a sheltered crack in a tree or rock to sleep the winter away.

◄ Many plants rest in winter too. As days begin to get shorter, deciduous trees start to prepare for the cold. Their leaves die and then fall to the ground. This helps trees and shrubs survive the cold weather. Deciduous trees may seem lifeless in winter but, on a closer look, you can see that they are covered in tight new leaf and flower buds. These will start to grow when the temperature rises in spring and the trees burst into life again.

LIFETIME

All living animals follow a cycle from birth (or hatching) through growth to death. Some will bear young, which will follow their own life cycles. But the life expectancies of different species can vary enormously.

▲ Most insects live for a very short time. A house fly hatches, becomes adult, lays eggs, and then dies within a month.

◄ Tiny mice are fed on their mother's milk for about three weeks. After this they will have to find their own food. Mice live for only about two years. In this time they will have many young.

◄ Asian elephants can live to be seventy years old. A baby elephant is fed by its mother for three or four years, but often it stays with her for much longer.

Turtles are some of the longest-living creatures on earth. They hatch from eggs laid in sandy beaches, find their way down to the shore, and then swim free in the sea. They can live for well over a hundred years.

This chart shows the longest recorded life spans of some animals.

30 days – Housefly

1 year – Monarch butterfly

2 years – Mouse

12 years – Rabbit

20 years – Dog

30 years – Cat

40 years – Swan

70 years – Elephant

119 years – Human

150 years – Tortoise

Plants have life spans too. Some–like marigolds–germinate, flower, produce seeds, and die within a few months. Others, like foxglove, need two years to complete a similar cycle. Some trees and shrubs live for many years, making flowers from new growth every summer.

WOW!
The oldest living thing on Earth is a bristlecone pine tree in the United States. It is almost 5,000 years old.

THE CHANGING MOON

The seasons make a poor clock for measuring the passing of a year. Spring sometimes arrives late and winter can come early. Thousands of years ago, people found a more accurate guide using the shape of the moon.

Just as the earth takes a year to travel around the sun, the moon orbits the earth every twenty-nine and a half days. In this time, it grows from a thin curve of light to a complete circle and back again. For a short period there is no moon to be seen at all. We call these changes the phases of the moon.

Many ancient peoples believed the moon was a cruel goddess—but they still used it as a clock. By watching its changes, they had the idea of dividing the year into weeks and months (the word comes from *moonths*). Twelve moons take roughly the same time that the seasons take to complete their cycle. By counting the moons, people could measure the passing of a year.

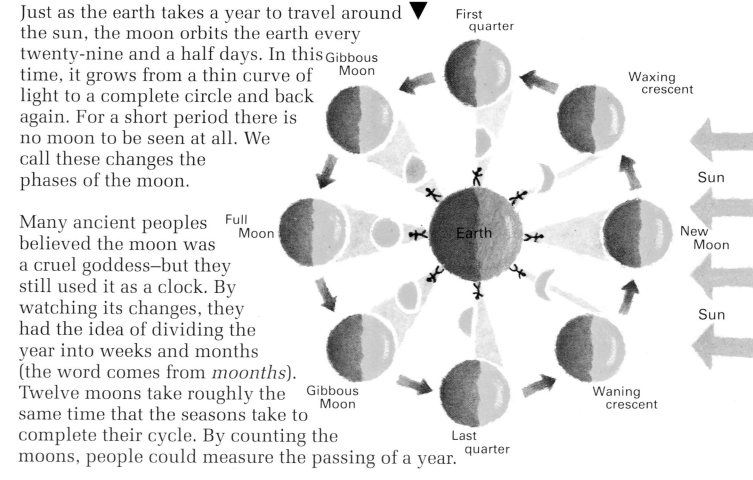

First quarter

Gibbous Moon

Waxing crescent

Sun

Full Moon

Earth

New Moon

Sun

Gibbous Moon

Waning crescent

Last quarter

TIME AND TIDES

In summer, many people go to the beach. Before they lay their towels out, they want to know whether the tide is in or out. Twice a day, as the tide rises, the sea covers the beach. Twice a day the sea falls and reveals the land again.

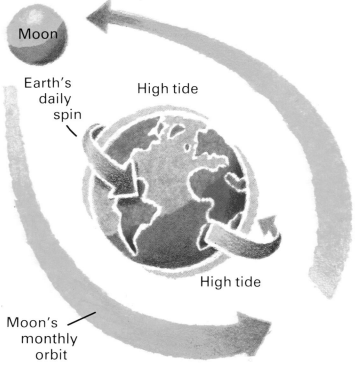

Moon

Earth's daily spin

High tide

High tide

Moon's monthly orbit

◀ Tides are caused mainly by the pull of the moon. All objects have a pull on one another, even if it is so weak that it can't be felt. Objects with more mass pull more strongly than those with less. The moon has a pull that is strong enough to make water in the earth's seas and oceans bulge towards it. It also pulls the earth away from the water on the opposite side of the world, forming another bulge. These two bulges are the twice-daily rising tides. They move around the earth in line with the moon.

The sun affects tides ▶ too. Very high and low tides occur when the sun and the moon are in line and pull together. When the sun and moon are at right angles to each other, they act against each other and there is less difference between the high and low tides.

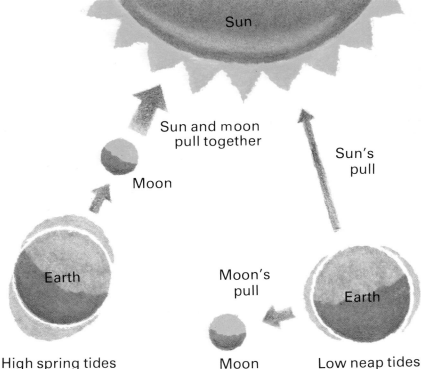

Sun

Sun and moon pull together

Moon

Sun's pull

Moon's pull

Earth

Earth

High spring tides

Moon

Low neap tides

EARLY CALENDARS

Although the changing moon is useful for tracking the passing year, people wanted something more accurate to plan their seasonal celebrations and crop-planting. They found ways to base an annual calendar on the sun or the pattern of the stars. Now there are many kinds of calendars in use all over the world. They often start at different times of the year. New Year is usually a time for celebration.

Following the regular patterns of the stars, or zodiac, gives a more reliable timing of the year. These patterns appear in the sky at the same time each year. Astronomers can use the zodiac to put lunar calendars back on course.

The ancient Egyptians used star time. They watched the movements of our brightest star, Syrius, in the night sky. As long ago as 4000 B.C. their calendar had 365 days in a year.

Moon—or lunar—calendars are complicated because a lunar year is slightly shorter than a solar year. The moon completes its twelve cycles in about 354 days, while the earth takes about 365 days to complete its orbit of the sun. Because the Muslim calendar is a true lunar calendar, months end up wandering through the seasons. The same month can be in summer one year and in winter a few years later.

◀ The Chinese follow a lunar calendar. They add a month from time to time so that New Year is always celebrated at some time between January 17 and February 19.

The Jewish calendar is based on the movements of both the moon and the sun. Most years follow a lunar year, and each year eleven days are lost. A thirteenth month has to be added in some years to bring time back on course with the solar year. ▶

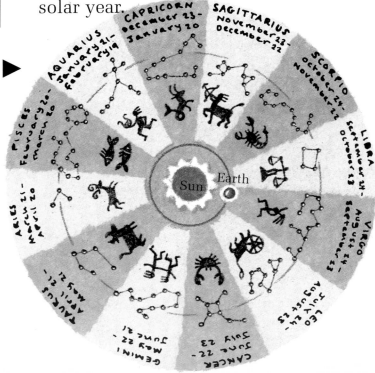

This Mexican temple was built with 365 little boxes around its walls. It is thought that each box belonged to the god of a day in the year. Offerings were probably made to each god in turn. In this way, the temple would also have acted as an early calendar.

What the early astronomers didn't know was that a solar year actually lasts about 365 1/4 days. This extra quarter of a day doesn't seem very much, but leaving it out of a calendar for a number of years would mean months eventually slipping into the wrong season.

In 46 B.C. Julius Caesar decided to straighten it all out. He introduced a new calendar that took care of this extra quarter day. Every four years an extra day was added and the year was called a leap year.

However, the calendar still gained days. So in the year 1582, Pope Gregory XIII ordered that that year ten days should be dropped. He also decided that from then on, the leap year should be skipped in the last year of every century unless that year could be divided by 400. This would keep the calendar straight for all time. The Gregorian calendar is still used all over the world today, although other calendars are used as well.

WOW!

People going to bed in the United States September 2, 1752, woke up on September 14 the next morning. They lost eleven days overnight when they finally changed from the Julian to the Georgian calendar.

MARKING TIME

"Eighty-five, ninety, ninety-five, one hundred. Coming, ready or not!" Most of us have played hide-and-seek. The seeker counts to give everybody else time to hide. This is a way of measuring time without a clock.

Hours, minutes, and seconds are an invention that help us to measure time. Before mechanical clocks were made, it wasn't always easy to tell how time was passing.

Sundials were first used at least 4,000 years ago, but they were only useful during daylight hours on sunny days. People needed something that could be used at any time of the day or night.

WOW!
Imagine counting all day. In some monasteries in the Middle Ages, monks chanted certain psalms at a steady rate. A fixed number of psalms told the hour.

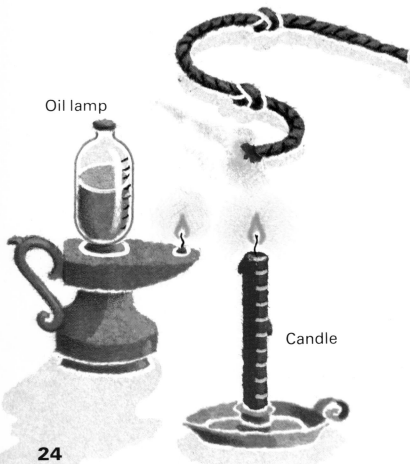

Knotted rope

Oil lamp

Candle

▲ One of the first timers was invented by the Chinese. They set fire to dampened ropes that were knotted at regular intervals. As the fire slowly burned past each knot, a period of time was counted off. Later, fire clocks were made to drop weights as the fire passed. The falling weights chimed the time.

◄ Candles and oil lamps were turned into simple fire clocks too. As they burned down, the time was told by reading the levels marked on them.

SAND AND WATER CLOCKS

The early Greeks and Romans used water to tell the time. A large bowl with a small hole in the bottom was filled with water. As the water trickled through, the falling water level uncovered markings inside the bowl. These told how time was passing.

The Chinese and Indians used water clocks that worked the other way around. A small brass bowl with a tiny hole was floated on top of the water. As the bowl filled up, the water covered markings on its side. When the bowl sank, a gong was struck and the bowl was emptied and floated again.

▲ This ancient Greek water clock was steadily filled by pipes. The level of water against the steps marked the time.

Water clocks, or clepsydra, became more and more complicated. In some, the escaping water turned wheels. In others, hours were told by pointing hands, ringing bells, beating drums, or sounding trumpets.

◀ When we want to soft boil an egg, we sometimes use a sandglass. As soon as the timer is turned upside-down the sand slips through its thin neck. Sandglasses can be very accurate. Some old sandglasses were made to measure quarter, half, or even whole hours.

Make a Sand Timer

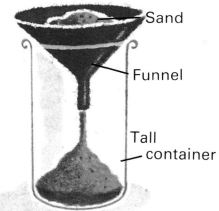

Sand

Funnel

Tall container

1 Using a funnel, a tall container, and some dry sand, experiment to make a timer that will run for three minutes.
2 Work out a way to mark the passing of time.

CLOCK WORK

The first mechanical clocks were made toward the end of the thirteenth century. Some had only one hand to point the hour. Others had no hands at all; instead the hours were struck on bells by jointed figures called Jacks.

▲ The life-sized Jacks of this clock in Venice, Italy, still stand ready to strike their bell.

Many of the early mechanical clocks were very big and heavy. They were powered by a falling weight which turned a drum to keep the clock going.

In 1550 a German locksmith named Peter Henlein discovered that a coiled steel spring could be used to drive clocks.

◀ Spring-driven clocks were smaller and lighter than those that used weights. Within fifty years, spring-driven clocks were made small enough for people to carry around. These watches were beautifully decorated and very expensive. People wore them on chains around their necks.

ALL WOUND UP

You can make a simple clock that uses the stored energy in a wound piece of string.

1 Cut out a window in the side of an open cardboard box.

2 Make two holes opposite each other –in the ends–to tightly fit a dowel rod through.

Rod

3 Fasten a piece of string to the rod with a tack. Put a large ball of clay on the other end.

4 Fix a pointer to one end of the rod. Draw a clock face on the box around the pointer.

5 Balance the box between two chairs.

6 Turn the rod to wind the string around it.

7 Let the rod go. Watch the hand spin as the clay unwinds the string.

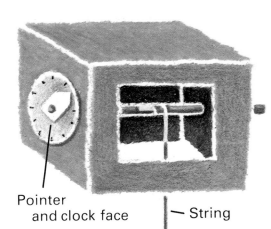

Pointer and clock face

String

Ball of clay

The hands of your clock will spin very fast. Most clocks ▶ use a mechanism called an escapement to slow down the release of stored energy. Since medieval times, many clocks use a toothed wheel as an escapement. A lever rocks up and down, catching and releasing the wheel. The wheel then lets the weight down in steps.

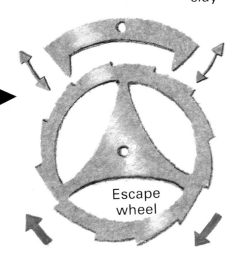

Escape wheel

You can add an escape wheel to your clock.

8 Carefully cut the top off a plastic bottle, making small zigzags around the edge.

9 Fit the neck of the bottle onto the rod and use some clay to attach it.

10 Rewind the string.

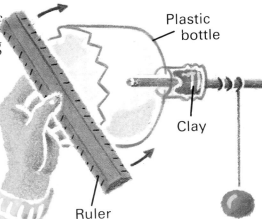

Plastic bottle

Clay

Ruler

11 Hold a ruler so that it catches first a tooth at the top then one at the bottom of the escape wheel to slow the movement down.

PENDULUMS

Soon after springs were first used in clocks, an Italian named Galileo discovered the properties of the pendulum. A pendulum is a rod or cable with a weight at the end. It swings backward and forward at a steady rate, making it an accurate mechanism for the timing in clocks.

Test a Pendulum

You can make a pendulum from a length of string and a ball of modeling clay.

1 Fix the clay to one end. Use a thumbtack to secure the other end above a doorway where it can swing freely.
2 Time how long it takes for the pendulum to swing both ways thirty times.
3 Make the clay ball heavier. Notice that this does not change your results.
4 Try shortening and lengthening the string. Notice that a longer string produces a slower swing.
5 Experiment to find the length of pendulum you need to make thirty double swings take exactly one minute. This will be the same length as a pendulum in a clock.

◄ A grandfather, or long case, clock has a pendulum swinging inside it. The pendulum is kept moving by the energy in a slowly falling weight. The movement of the pendulum works the machinery that turns the clock's hands.

PERFECT TIMING

Many modern clocks and watches are powered by electricity. Inside they have a tiny battery and a quartz crystal. When electricity from the battery passes through the crystal, it vibrates thousands of times each second. The vibrations are so regular that the clock or watch keeps very good time.

Quartz clocks sometimes have a dial and hands to show the time, but many have a digital display. This shows the time in numbers. Digital clocks have no moving parts. Instead, a microchip counts the vibrations from the quartz crystal and sends out a signal to change the numbers on the display as the time passes.

▲ Quartz clocks and watches can measure fractions of a second. They are used by athletes to time their races. Records can be set by as little as one hundredth of a second.

◀ Astronomers, and other scientists who need to measure time precisely, use atomic clocks. These are accurate to one second in 3,000 years. It is difficult to imagine a clock more accurate than this.

GLOSSARY

Astronomer A scientist who studies the stars and planets.

Atomic clock A clock that uses the natural vibrations of the very tiniest parts of matter which makes it extremely accurate.

Axis An imaginary line that runs straight through the center of the earth from the North Pole to the South. The earth spins around its axis.

Crystal A substance, the faces of which are arranged in a regular pattern.

Deciduous Trees that lose all their leaves for the winter.

Digital Shown in the form of numerals.

Echo-location The ability to find objects by using reflected sounds.

Escapement The mechanism in a clock that controls the release of energy that drives the pendulum.

Gorge A deep, wide valley.

Hemispheres Two halves of a globe.

Hibernation A deep sleep that some animals fall into to get them through the winter.

Lunar year The time it takes for the moon to complete twelve phases.

Magnetic field The invisible lines of force around the earth that run roughly from the North to the South poles.

Microchip A tiny piece of silicon that is printed with lots of information for use inside computers, calculators, and watches.

Migrate To move from one place to another.

Nectar A sweet, sticky substance produced by a flower to attract insects.

Orbit The circular path followed by something as it travels around an object or planet.

Solar year The time it takes for the earth to orbit the sun. It is sometimes called a calendar year.

Species A particular kind of animal or plant.

Sundial A clock that uses shadows cast by the sun to measure the passage of time.

Tide The daily rise and fall of the seas.

Vibrate To shake rapidly.

BOOKS TO READ

There are lots of topics in this book for you to explore further. Here are just a few suggestions for books to read to get you started:

Adler, Irving. *Time in Your Life.* New York: John Day, 1969

Adler, Irving and Ruth. *The Calendar.* New York: John Day, 1967

Apfel, Necia H. *Calendars.* New York: Franklin Watts, 1985

Bell, Thelma Harrington and Corydon Bell. *The Riddle of Time.* New York: Viking Press, 1963

Berger, Melvin. *Time After Time.* New York: Coward, McCann & Geoghegan, 1975

Burns, Marilyn. *This Book Is about Time.* Boston: Little, Brown, 1978

Galt, Tom. *Seven Days from Sunday.* New York: Thomas Y. Crowell, 1956

Jespersen, James and Jane Fitz-Randolph. *Time & Clocks.* New York: Atheneum, 1979

Johnson, Timothy. *River of Time.* New York: Coward-McCann, 1967

Marchall, Roy K. *Sandials.* New York: Macmillan, 1963

Silverberg, Robert. *Clocks for the Ages: How Scientists Date the Past.* New York: Macmillan 1971

Sims, Jean and Michael Connelly. *Time and Space.* Englewood Cliffs, N.J.: Prentice-Hall, 1982

INDEX